This virus makes me angry!

 There is a virus called coronavirus that is making a lot of people sick.

A virus is a type of germ. A germ is so tiny that you need a microscope to see it. When a germ gets inside your body it can make you sick.

Doctors, nurses, and other healthcare workers are helping people stay healthy and safe.

Scientists around the world are working to help fight the virus and find a vaccine. Do you know what a vaccine is?

This is why school is going to be a little different this year. Sometimes we will be in our classroom.

Sometimes we will have to stay home and see our friends and teachers through the computer.

While we are at school, we need to follow new rules that will keep our friends and teachers healthy.

You can help be a germ-fighting superhero at school by following five easy rules.

1 WASH YOUR HANDS

The most important thing you can do to keep germs away is to wash your hands.

Use soap and water and rub your hands until you make bubbles. Wash your hands for at least 20 seconds. Let's count!

Sometimes if you don't have soap it's okay to use hand sanitizer. That will also help fight germs.

When else do you think we should wash our hands at school?

Wearing a mask helps keep germs to yourself. It is one way to help the virus from spreading to friends and teachers.

The mask needs to cover your nose and mouth. Try not to touch your mask.

Your friends and teachers will be wearing one too. Don't worry, everyone is still smiling even though you can't see it.

We will still play games, read stories, make new friends, and have fun at school.

We have to give our friends their own space bubble.

Even though we love high fives and hugs, we need to think of new ways to greet our teachers and friends.

wave hello!
elbow bump!
Do a dance!
What other ways can you greet your teachers and friends?

Can you show me how you cover your sneeze and cough?

Tell your teacher if you feel warm or if your head or stomach hurts.

You might have your temperature taken to see if you have a fever.

Now you know the five ways you can be a germ-fighting superhero at school.

Remember that school won't always be like this, but for now it is the best way to keep our friends and teachers healthy.

Made in the USA
Coppell, TX
01 October 2020